BEST OF
SPAIN

Consultant Editor:
Valerie Ferguson

HERMES HOUSE

Contents

Introduction

Eating is a serious, but enjoyable business in Spain. The day usually begins early with coffee and a pastry, then a light lunch – *almuerzo* – follows in the late morning before the sun is too hot for eating. The main meal of the day – *comida* – is served in the mid-afternoon and usually consists of at least three courses. This is traditionally followed by a siesta until the cool of the early evening. When work has finished, it is time to relax with a glass of chilled sherry and a few tapas dishes. The day ends with a light supper in the late evening.

Tapas originated in Andalucia in southern Spain, but are now popular in dozens of other countries. A tapa is a lid, so called because sherry was served with the glass covered with a slice of bread topped with ham or cheese to keep out the flies. Tapas are designed to be easy to eat, usually with the fingers or speared on cocktail sticks. Although intended as snacks, an entire meal – vegetarian or mixed – can be constructed from a selection of six or more different tapas dishes.

This book includes the classic dishes, from chilled soups to paella, from tapas to meat casseroles, with refreshing desserts, which make the most of Spain's luscious fruits, to follow.

Ingredients

Spanish food is a delight to the eye and the palate, using a variety of fresh ingredients and aromatic flavourings.

Dairy Products: Both milk and cream feature in desserts, but are not so widely used in savoury dishes. The best-known Spanish cheese is Manchego, from La Mancha, made from ewe's milk. Young Manchego, which is soft and creamy, is difficult to find outside Spain, but the tangy, full-flavoured mature cheese is widely available.

Fish & Seafood: Hake, fresh sardines and salt cod, *bacalao*, are among the most popular fish in Spain and other favourites include anchovies, monkfish and mullet. Other popular seafood includes mussels, clams, prawns, squid, crab and lobster.

Fruit: Spain is rich in fruit, particularly oranges, lemons, figs, peaches and melons, and is a large commercial producer of strawberries.

Grains & Pulses: The ideal rice for paella is Valencia rice, but as it may be difficult to obtain outside Spain, Italian risotto or long grain rice can be used instead. Plain boiled or saffron-flavoured rice is a common accompaniment to meat and seafood dishes. Cornmeal, made from the abundant sweetcorn grown all over Spain, and many varieties of dried beans and peas often feature in Spanish soups and stews.

Above, anticlockwise from top: Garlic, saffron strands and paprika are essential flavourings.

Herbs & Spices: Garlic is a popular flavouring throughout Spain and features prominently in a number of tapas. Flat leaf parsley is popular both for flavour and as a garnish. Saffron consists of the dark orange stigmas from crocus flowers, and La Mancha is said to produce the best in the world. Paprika is a mild seasoning made from ground red pepper that can be used to add flavour and colour to many Spanish dishes.

Meat & Poultry: Pork is the country's most popular meat and beef, mostly in the form of steak, is frequently served in city restaurants and in the north of the country. Chicken – both whole and in cuts – is prepared in a wide variety of ways throughout Spain. Other favourites include duck and game; *Jamón serrano,* a raw, salt-cured rosy pink ham a little like prosciutto; *Chorizo,* a pork sausage flavoured with paprika, and black pudding, which is an important ingredient all over Spain.

Above, from left: Picos Blue, Manchego and Monte Enebro cheeses.

Nuts: Many varieties of nuts, especially almonds, grow abundantly in Spain, but they tend to be eaten as snacks and simple tapas, rather than incorporated into cooked dishes. Some traditional desserts are flavoured or decorated with almonds or pine nuts, and they are popular fillings and toppings for pastries.

Vegetables: Strictly speaking, olives are a fruit, but are used as a vegetable. Where possible, choose olives with their stones and pit them yourself. Those sold loose in brine are better than the ones packed in oil. Spanish onions have a sweet, mild flavour and are usually quite large. Other popular vegetables include green beans, courgettes, potatoes, spinach, peppers, sweetcorn and tomatoes.

Techniques

Stoning Olives

Pre-stoned olives lack the flavour and variety of whole ones, so stone them yourself if you can.

1 To remove the stone from an olive put the olive in the stoner, pointed end uppermost.

2 Squeeze the handles of the stoner together to extract the stone. Using a stoner is the easiest way to remove the stone from an olive, but you can also use a sharp knife.

Skinning & Chopping Tomatoes

It is sometimes recommended that you peel tomatoes before using them. Always use fully ripe tomatoes for the best flavour.

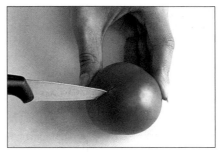

1 Using a small, sharp knife, cut a cross just through the skin at the base of each ripe tomato.

2 Put the tomatoes in a bowl and pour over boiling water. Leave for 20–30 seconds until the skin splits. Drain and transfer to a bowl of cold water. Peel off the skin and chop the flesh into even-size pieces.

Chopping Herbs

Chop herbs just before you use them: the flavour will then be at its best.

1 Place the leaves on a clean, dry board. Use a large, sharp cook's knife (if you use a blunt knife you will bruise the herbs rather than slice them) and chop them until as coarse or as fine as needed.

2 Alternatively, use a herb chopper, also called a *mezzaluna,* which is a very useful tool for finely chopping herbs or vegetables and consists of a sharp, curved blade with two handles. Use the *mezzaluna* in a see-saw motion for best results.

Preparing Garlic

Don't worry if you don't have a garlic press: try this method, which gives wonderfully juicy results.

1 Break off the clove of garlic, place the flat side of a large knife on top and strike with your fist. Remove all the papery outer skin. Begin by finely chopping the clove.

2 Sprinkle over a little table salt and, using the flat side of a large knife blade, work the salt into the garlic, until the clove softens and releases its juices. Use as required.

Spiced Potatoes

This is a peppery potato dish, of which there are several versions. All of them are fried and spiced with the added tang of wine vinegar.

Serves 4

INGREDIENTS
675 g/1½ lb unpeeled small
   new potatoes
salt
75 ml/5 tbsp olive oil
2 garlic cloves, sliced
2.5 ml/½ tsp crushed dried chillies
2.5 ml/½ tsp ground cumin
10 ml/2 tsp paprika
30 ml/2 tbsp red or white wine vinegar
1 red or green pepper, seeded
   and sliced
coarse sea salt,
   to serve (optional)

1 Cook the potatoes in boiling salted water until almost tender. Drain and, if preferred, peel them. Cut into chunks.

COOK'S TIP: Leaving the skins on the potatoes helps retain flavour and makes a good texture when fried.

2 Heat the oil in a large frying or sauté pan and fry the potatoes, turning them frequently, until golden.

3 Meanwhile, crush together the garlic, chillies and cumin using a pestle and mortar. Mix with the paprika and wine vinegar.

4 Add the garlic mixture to the potatoes with the sliced pepper and cook, stirring, for 2 minutes. Serve warm, or leave until cold. Scatter with coarse sea salt, if you like, to serve.

Marinated Pimientos

Pimientos are simply cooked, skinned peppers. You can buy them in cans or jars, but they are much tastier when home-made.

Serves 2–4

INGREDIENTS
3 red peppers
2 small garlic cloves, crushed
45 ml/3 tbsp chopped
   fresh parsley
15 ml/1 tbsp sherry vinegar
30 ml/2 tbsp olive oil
salt

2 When the peppers are cool enough to handle, make a small cut in the bottom of each pepper, squeeze out the juice into a jug and set aside. Peel away and discard the skin and cut both peppers in half lengthways, using a sharp knife. Remove and discard the core and seeds.

1 Preheat the grill to high. Place the peppers on a baking sheet and grill, turning occasionally, for 8–12 minutes, until the skins have blistered and blackened. Remove the peppers from the heat, cover with a clean dish towel and leave for 5 minutes so that the steam softens the skin.

COOK'S TIP: Red peppers are actually fully ripened green peppers. Buy firm, bright fruit and store refrigerated. Use as fresh as possible for the best flavour.

3 Cut the pepper halves into 1 cm/ ½ in wide strips and place them in a small bowl.

VARIATION: You could use a mixture of red and yellow peppers for this dish.

4 Whisk the garlic, parsley, vinegar and oil into the pepper juices. Add salt to taste. Pour over the pepper strips and toss well. Cover and chill, but, if possible, bring the peppers back to room temperature before serving.

Spinach with Pine Nuts

Raisins and pine nuts are frequent partners in Spanish recipes. Here, tossed with spinach and croûtons, they make a delicious snack or accompaniment.

Serves 4

INGREDIENTS
50 g/2 oz/⅓ cup raisins
1 thick slice white bread
45 ml/3 tbsp olive oil
25 g/1 oz/¼ cup pine nuts
500 g/1¼ lb young spinach, rinsed and
    stalks removed
2 garlic cloves, crushed
salt and freshly ground
    black pepper

1 Put the raisins in a small bowl, cover with boiling water and leave to soak for 10 minutes. Drain.

2 For the croûtons, cut the bread into cubes discarding the crusts. Heat 30 ml/2 tbsp of the oil and fry the bread until golden, turning frequently. Remove from the pan and drain.

3 Heat the remaining oil in the pan. Fry the pine nuts until beginning to colour. Add the spinach and garlic and cook quickly, turning the spinach until it has just wilted.

4 Toss in the raisins and season lightly with salt and pepper. Transfer to a warmed serving dish. Scatter with the croûtons and serve hot.

Tomato & Garlic Bread

A basket of warm, crusty, garlic-flavoured bread is a compulsory addition to any tapas table.

Serves 4-6

INGREDIENTS
4 large, ripe tomatoes, roughly chopped
2 garlic cloves, roughly chopped
1.5 ml/¼ tsp sea salt
grated rind and juice of ½ lemon
5 ml/1 tsp light brown sugar
1 flat loaf of bread, such as country bread
30 ml/2 tbsp olive oil
freshly ground black pepper

1 Preheat the oven to 200°C/400°F/ Gas 6. Place the tomatoes, garlic, salt, lemon rind and brown sugar in a small saucepan. Cover and cook over a low heat for 5 minutes.

2 Cut the loaf in half horizontally, then cut each half widthways into two to three pieces. Place on a baking sheet and bake for 5-8 minutes, until hot, crisp and golden brown.

3 Meanwhile, stir the lemon juice and olive oil into the tomato mixture. Cook, uncovered, for 8 minutes more, until the mixture is thick and pulpy.

4 Spoon the tomato mixture on the hot bread, sprinkle with pepper and serve at once.

Classic Potato Tortilla

A traditional Spanish tortilla contains potatoes and onions. Other ingredients can be added, but it is generally accepted that the classic tortilla cannot be improved upon.

Serves 6

INGREDIENTS
450 g/1 lb small waxy potatoes
1 Spanish onion
45 ml/3 tbsp vegetable oil
4 eggs
salt and freshly ground
    black pepper
flat leaf parsley, to garnish

2 Heat 30 ml/2 tbsp of the oil in a 20 cm/8 in heavy-based frying pan. Add the potatoes and onion and cook, stirring frequently, over a low heat for about 10 minutes, until the potatoes are just tender. Remove from the heat.

3 In a large bowl, beat together the eggs with a little salt and pepper. Stir in the sliced potatoes and onion.

1 With a sharp knife, peel the potatoes and slice them thinly. Slice the onion thinly and separate the slices into rings.

VARIATION: Tortilla is also good cold and makes an excellent packed lunch or picnic dish.

4 Heat the remaining oil in the frying pan and pour in the potato mixture. Cook very gently for 5–8 minutes, until the mixture is almost set.

5 Place a large plate upside-down over the pan, invert the tortilla on to the plate and then slide it back into the pan. Cook for 2–3 minutes more, until the underside of the tortilla is golden brown. Cut into wedges and serve garnished with flat leaf parsley.

Salt Cod Fish Cakes with Aïoli

Bite-size fish cakes, dipped in a rich garlic mayonnaise, are irresistible. Start these in good time, as the salt cod needs lengthy soaking.

Serves 6

INGREDIENTS
450 g/1 lb potatoes, peeled and cubed
115 g/4 oz salt cod, soaked in cold water,
    changed three times, for 48 hours
15 ml/1 tbsp olive oil
1 small onion, finely chopped
2 garlic cloves, finely chopped
30 ml/2 tbsp chopped fresh parsley
1 egg, beaten
Tabasco or chilli sauce
plain flour, for dusting
vegetable oil, for frying
salt and freshly ground black pepper
flat leaf parsley and lemon wedges,
    to garnish
aïoli, to serve

1 Cook the potatoes in a saucepan of boiling water for 10–12 minutes, until tender. Drain well, then mash until smooth. Set aside.

2 Place the cod in a frying pan, add water to cover and bring to the boil. Drain the fish, then remove the skin and bones. Using a fork, break the flesh into small pieces.

3 Heat the olive oil in a small saucepan and cook the onion and garlic for 5 minutes, until softened.

4 In a large bowl, mix together the mashed potato, flaked fish, fried onion mixture and parsley. Bind with the egg, then add salt, pepper and Tabasco or chilli sauce to taste. With floured hands, shape the mixture into 18 small balls.

5 Flatten the balls slightly and place on a large floured plate. Chill for about 15 minutes.

COOK'S TIP: To make aïoli, put four or more crushed garlic cloves in a bowl with a pinch of salt and crush with the back of a spoon. Add two egg yolks and beat with an electric mixer for 30 seconds, until creamy. Gradually beat in 250 ml/8 fl oz/1 cup extra virgin olive oil, adding it in drops. As the aïoli begins to thicken, add the oil in a constant stream. Thin the sauce with a little lemon juice and season to taste.

6 Heat 1 cm/½ in vegetable oil in a large frying pan. Cook the fish cakes for 3–4 minutes on each side until golden. Drain on kitchen paper and serve hot, garnished with parsley and lemon wedges and accompanied by the aïoli.

Sizzling Prawns

This delicious dish takes almost no time to prepare. Serve immediately, while still sizzling – you can serve it straight from the pan, if you like.

Serves 4

INGREDIENTS
2 garlic cloves, halved
25 g/1 oz/2 tbsp butter
1 small red chilli, seeded and finely sliced
115 g/4 oz cooked prawns, in the shell
sea salt and coarsely ground black pepper
lime wedges, to serve

1 Rub the cut surfaces of the halved garlic cloves over the surface of a frying pan then throw them away. Add the butter to the pan and melt over a fairly high heat until it just begins to turn golden brown.

2 Toss in the chilli and prawns. Stir-fry for 1–2 minutes, until heated through, then season to taste and serve with lime wedges to squeeze over.

Fried Squid

The squid is simply dusted in flour and dipped in egg before being fried, so the coating is light and does not mask the flavour.

Serves 4

INGREDIENTS
115 g/4 oz prepared squid, cut into rings
30 ml/2 tbsp seasoned flour
1 egg
30 ml/2 tbsp milk
olive oil, for frying
sea salt
lemon wedges, to serve

1 Toss the squid rings in the seasoned flour in a bowl or strong plastic bag. Beat the egg and milk together in a shallow bowl. Heat the oil in a heavy-based frying pan.

2 Dip the floured squid rings, one at a time, into the egg mixture, shaking off any excess liquid. Add to the hot oil, in batches if necessary, and fry for 2–3 minutes on each side, until golden.

3 Drain the fried squid on kitchen paper, then sprinkle with salt. Transfer to a small warm plate and serve with the lemon wedges.

VARIATION: For a crisper coating, dust the rings in flour, then dip them in batter instead of this simple egg and flour coating.

Green Beans with Ham

This is a popular combination and is also prepared with *lomo ahumado*,
cured and smoked loin of pork, or *tocino*, a very fatty bacon.

Serves 4

INGREDIENTS
450 g/1 lb French beans
45 ml/3 tbsp olive oil
1 onion, thinly sliced
2 garlic cloves, finely chopped
75 g/3 oz/½ cup chopped
    jamón serrano
salt and freshly ground
    black pepper

1 Cook the French beans in boiling,
lightly salted water for 5–6 minutes,
until just tender, but still with a
little bite. Drain well.

2 Meanwhile, heat the oil in a frying
pan, add the onion and fry for about
5 minutes, until softened and
translucent. Add the garlic and ham
and cook for a further 1–2 minutes.

3 Add the beans to the pan and cook,
stirring occasionally, for 2–3 minutes.
Season to taste with salt and pepper
and serve hot.

COOK'S TIP: *Jamón serrano*, literally
"mountain ham", generally comes
from the Caceres, Granada and
Salamanca regions of Spain.

Stewed Beans & Pork

Fabada is a classic Spanish stew which takes its name from a type of white bean. This is a simple, speedy version that serves very well as tapas.

Serves 4

INGREDIENTS
15 ml/1 tbsp olive oil
175 g/6 oz belly pork, rind removed
 and diced
115 g/4 oz cured chorizo sausage, diced
1 onion, chopped
2 garlic cloves, finely chopped
1 large tomato, roughly chopped
1.5 ml/¼ tsp dried chilli flakes
400 g/14 oz can cannellini
 beans, drained
150 ml/¼ pint/⅔ cup chicken stock
salt and freshly ground black pepper
flat leaf parsley, to garnish

1 Heat the oil in a large frying pan and fry the pork, chorizo, onion and garlic for 5–10 minutes, until the onion has softened and browned. Add the tomato and chilli flakes and cook for 1 minute more.

2 Stir in the beans and stock. Bring to the boil, lower the heat, cover and simmer for 15–20 minutes, until the pork is cooked through. Add salt and pepper to taste and serve, garnished with parsley.

Gazpacho

A traditional, chilled soup, perfect for a summer lunch. Make sure all the ingredients are in peak condition for the best-flavoured soup.

Serves 6

INGREDIENTS
1 green pepper, seeded and
    roughly chopped
1 red pepper, seeded and
    roughly chopped
½ cucumber, roughly chopped
1 onion, roughly chopped
1 fresh red chilli, seeded and
    roughly chopped
450 g/1 lb ripe plum tomatoes,
    roughly chopped
900 ml/1½ pints/3¾ cups passata or
    tomato juice
30 ml/2 tbsp red wine vinegar
30 ml/2 tbsp olive oil
15 ml/1 tbsp caster sugar
salt and freshly ground black pepper
crushed ice, to garnish (optional)

1 Reserve small pieces of green and red pepper, cucumber and onion, finely chop and set aside as a garnish.

2 Process all the remaining ingredients (except the ice) in a blender or food processor until smooth. You may need to do this in several batches.

3 Pass the soup through a strainer into a clean glass bowl, pushing it through with a spoon to extract as much flavour as possible.

VARIATION: If liked, serve fried bread croûtons and chopped black olives in bowls for adding to the soup.

4 Adjust the seasoning and chill. Serve the gazpacho sprinkled with the reserved chopped peppers, cucumber and onion. For an extra special touch, add a little crushed ice to the garnish if liked.

Galician Broth

This delicious, hearty soup is very similar to the warming, chunky meat and potato broths of cooler climates.

Serves 4

INGREDIENTS

450 g/1 lb gammon, in one piece
2 bay leaves
2 onions, sliced
10 ml/2 tsp paprika
675 g/1½ lb potatoes, peeled and cut into
  large chunks
225 g/8 oz spring greens
425 g/15 oz can haricot or
  cannellini beans, drained
salt and freshly ground
  black pepper

1 Soak the gammon overnight in cold water. Drain and put into a large saucepan with the bay leaves and onions. Pour over 1.5 litres/2½ pints/6¼ cups fresh cold water.

2 Bring to the boil, then reduce the heat and simmer very gently for about 1½ hours, until the meat is tender. Keep an eye on the pan to make sure it doesn't boil over.

VARIATION: Bacon knuckles can be used instead of the gammon. The bones will give the cooking liquid a delicious flavour.

3 Drain the meat, reserving the cooking liquid, and cool slightly. Discard the skin and any excess fat from the meat and cut into chunks.

4 Return to the pan with the reserved cooking liquid, the paprika and potatoes. Bring to the boil then reduce the heat, cover and simmer gently for 15 minutes.

5 Cut away the cores from the greens. Roll up the leaves and cut into thin shreds. Add to the pan with the beans and simmer for about 5–10 minutes. Season with salt and pepper to taste and serve hot.

Chilled Tomato & Sweet Pepper Soup

Unlike Gazpacho, this soup is cooked before being chilled.

Serves 4

INGREDIENTS
2 red peppers, halved and seeded
45 ml/3 tbsp olive oil
1 onion, finely chopped
2 garlic cloves, crushed
675 g/1½ lb ripe well-flavoured tomatoes,
    cut into chunks
150 ml/¼ pint/⅔ cup red wine
600 ml/1 pint/2½ cups chicken stock
salt and freshly ground
    black pepper
snipped fresh chives, to garnish

FOR THE CROUTONS
60 ml/4 tbsp olive oil
2 slices white bread, crusts removed
    and cut into cubes

1 Preheat the grill. Cut each pepper half into quarters. Place skin side up on a grill rack and cook until the skins have charred. Transfer to a bowl and cover with a plate until cool.

2 Heat the oil in a large saucepan. Add the onion and garlic and cook until soft.

COOK'S TIP: If picking home-grown chives only use the tender non-flowering leaves.

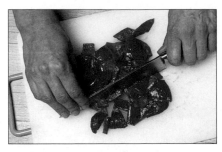

3 When cool enough to handle, remove and discard the skin from the peppers and chop the flesh.

4 Add the peppers and tomatoes to the pan, then cover and cook gently for 10 minutes. Add the wine and cook for a further 5 minutes, then add the stock and salt and pepper and continue to simmer for 20 minutes.

5 To make the croûtons, heat the oil in a small frying pan, add the bread and fry until golden. Drain on kitchen paper and store in an airtight box.

6 Process the soup in a blender or food processor until smooth. Pour into a clean glass or ceramic bowl and leave to cool thoroughly before chilling in the fridge for at least 3 hours. When the soup is cold, season to taste. Serve the soup in bowls, topped with the croûtons and garnished with chives.

Garlic Soup

This is a simple and satisfying soup, made with one of the most popular ingredients in Spain – garlic!

Serves 4

INGREDIENTS
30 ml/2 tbsp olive oil
4 large garlic cloves
4 slices French bread,
   5 mm/¼ in thick
15 ml/1 tbsp paprika
1 litre/1¾ pints/4 cups
   beef stock
1.5 ml/¼ tsp ground cumin
pinch of saffron strands
4 eggs
salt and freshly ground
   black pepper
chopped fresh parsley,
   to garnish

1 Preheat the oven to 230°C/450°F/ Gas 8. Heat the oil in a saucepan. Add the garlic cloves and cook until golden. Remove and set aside. Fry the bread until golden, then set aside.

2 Add the paprika to the pan, and fry for a few seconds. Stir in the stock, cumin, saffron and the reserved garlic, crushing the cloves with the back of a spoon. Season, then cook for 5 minutes.

3 Ladle the soup into four ovenproof bowls and break an egg into each. Top each with a slice of fried bread and place in the oven for 3–4 minutes, until the eggs are set. Serve sprinkled with parsley.

Chilled Almond Soup

Unless you want to spend time pounding the ingredients for this dish by hand, a food processor is essential.

Serves 6

INGREDIENTS
115 g/4 oz fresh white bread, about
    4 thick slices
115 g/4 oz/1 cup blanched almonds
2 garlic cloves, sliced
75 ml/5 tbsp olive oil
25 ml/1½ tbsp sherry vinegar
salt and freshly ground
    black pepper
toasted flaked almonds and
    seedless green and black
    grapes, halved and peeled,
    to garnish

1 Break the bread into a bowl and pour over 150 ml/¼ pint/⅔ cup cold water. Leave for 5 minutes.

2 Put the almonds and garlic in a blender or food processor and process until very finely ground. Blend in the soaked white bread and water.

3 Gradually add the oil until the mixture forms a smooth paste. Add the sherry vinegar then 600 ml/1 pint/2½ cups cold water and process until completely smooth.

4 Transfer to a bowl and season with salt and pepper, adding a little more water if the soup is very thick. Chill for at least 2–3 hours.

5 Ladle the soup into bowls and scatter with the toasted almonds and peeled grapes.

Pan-fried Garlic Sardines

Lightly fried sardines with a hint of garlic make a delicious lunch or supper. This dish could also be made with fresh anchovies if available.

Serves 4

INGREDIENTS
1.2 kg/2½ lb fresh sardines
30 ml/2 tbsp olive oil
4 garlic cloves
finely grated rind of 2 lemons
30 ml/2 tbsp chopped
  fresh parsley
salt and freshly ground
  black pepper
fried garlic slices, to garnish

FOR THE TOMATO TOAST
2 large ripe beefsteak tomatoes
8 slices crusty bread, toasted

1 Gut and clean the sardines thoroughly. If preferred, you can remove their heads, but this is not essential. Scale the fish, by gently scraping along the length of the body from the tail to head with a scaling knife or your hand. This is best done under cold running water.

2 Heat the oil in a frying pan and add the garlic cloves. Cook over a low heat until soft. Remove and set aside.

3 Add the sardines and fry for 4–5 minutes. Sprinkle over some of the lemon rind, parsley and seasoning.

VARIATION: If you are lucky enough to find fresh anchovies, which are very much smaller than sardines, prepare them by bending and snapping the backbone behind the head. As you pull the head away, most of the guts are removed with it.

4 Crush the whole garlic cloves and spread on the toast. Cut the tomatoes in half and rub them on to the toast, discarding the skins. Serve the sardines accompanied by the tomato toast, and garnished with the fried garlic slices, remaining parsley and lemon rind.

Hake with White Wine

In Spain, hake is an immensely popular fish. Its flesh has a delicate flavour and a fragile texture.

Serves 4

INGREDIENTS
30 ml/2 tbsp olive oil
25 g/1 oz/2 tbsp butter
1 onion, chopped
3 garlic cloves, chopped
15 ml/1 tbsp plain flour
2.5 ml/½ tsp paprika
4 hake cutlets, about 175 g/6 oz each
250 g/9 oz/2 cups fine green beans, cut into
    2.5 cm/1 in lengths
350 ml/12 fl oz/1½ cups fish stock
150 ml/¼ pint/⅔ cup dry white wine
30 ml/2 tbsp dry sherry
16–20 fresh mussels, debearded
    and scrubbed
45 ml/3 tbsp chopped fresh parsley
salt and freshly ground black pepper
crusty bread, to serve

2 Mix together the flour and paprika, then lightly dust over the hake cutlets. Push the onion and garlic to one side of the pan. Add the hake cutlets to the pan and fry for 5 minutes on each side, until golden.

3 Stir in the beans, stock, wine, sherry and seasoning. Bring to the boil and cook for about 2 minutes.

COOK'S TIP: Before cooking the mussels discard any that do not close when lightly tapped.

1 Heat the oil and butter in a frying pan, add the onion and cook for 5 minutes, until softened, but not browned. Add the chopped garlic and cook for 1 minute more.

4 Add the mussels and parsley, cover the pan and cook for 5–8 minutes, until the mussels have opened. Discard any mussels that remain closed. Serve the hake in warmed, shallow soup bowls with crusty bread to mop up the juices.

Seafood Paella

This is probably the best-known Spanish dish in the world. If you can't find Valencia rice, arborio rice makes a good substitute.

Serves 4

INGREDIENTS
60 ml/4 tbsp olive oil
225 g/8 oz monkfish or cod, skinned and
    cut into chunks
3 prepared baby squid, body cut into rings
    and tentacles chopped
1 red mullet, filleted, skinned and cut into
    chunks (optional)
1 onion, chopped
3 garlic cloves, finely chopped
1 red pepper, seeded and sliced
4 tomatoes, peeled and chopped
225 g/8 oz/1¼ cups Valencia rice
450 ml/¾ pint/scant 2 cups
    fish stock
150 ml/¼ pint/⅔ cup white wine
75 g/3 oz/¾ cup frozen peas
4–5 saffron strands soaked in 30 ml/2 tbsp
    hot water
115 g/4 oz/1 cup cooked peeled prawns
8 fresh mussels in shells, debearded
    and scrubbed
salt and freshly ground black pepper
15 ml/1 tbsp chopped fresh parsley,
    to garnish
lemon wedges, to serve

1 Heat 30 ml/2 tbsp of the olive oil in a large frying pan and add the monkfish or cod, squid and red mullet, if using. Stir-fry for 2 minutes, then transfer the fish with all the juices to a bowl and reserve.

2 Heat the remaining 30 ml/2 tbsp of oil in a sauté pan and add the onion, garlic and pepper. Fry, stirring frequently, for 6–7 minutes, until the onion and pepper have softened.

3 Stir in the tomatoes and fry for 2 minutes, then add the rice, stirring to coat the grains with oil, and cook for 2–3 minutes. Pour on the fish stock and wine and add the peas, saffron and water. Season well and mix.

4 Gently stir in the reserved cooked fish with all the juices, followed by the prawns, and then push the mussels into the rice.

5 Cover and cook, stirring occasionally, over a low heat for about 30 minutes, or until the stock has been absorbed but the mixture is still moist.

6 Remove from the heat, keep covered and leave to stand for 5 minutes. Discard any mussels that remain closed.

7 Garnish the paella with parsley and serve with lemon wedges.

COOK'S TIP: In Spain the dish is cooked in and served from a two-handled pan called a *paella*.

Hake & Clams with Salsa Verde

Here the ever-popular hake is cooked in a sauce flavoured with parsley, lemon juice and garlic.

Serves 4

INGREDIENTS
4 hake steaks, about 2 cm/¾ in thick
30 ml/2 tbsp plain flour for dusting,
    plus 30 ml/2 tbsp
60 ml/4 tbsp olive oil
15 ml/1 tbsp lemon juice
1 small onion,
    finely chopped
4 garlic cloves, crushed
150 ml/¼ pint/⅔ cup
    fish stock
150 ml/¼ pint/⅔ cup white wine
90 ml/6 tbsp chopped
    fresh parsley
75 g/3 oz/¾ cup frozen
    petits pois
8 fresh clams
salt and freshly ground
    black pepper

1 Preheat the oven to 180°C/350°F/ Gas 4. Season the hake steaks with salt and pepper, then dust both sides with flour.

2 Heat 30 ml/2 tbsp of the oil in a large sauté pan, add the fish and fry for about 1 minute on each side. Transfer to an ovenproof dish and sprinkle with lemon juice.

3 Clean the pan, then heat the remaining oil. Add the onion and garlic and cook until soft.

4 Stir in 30 ml/2 tbsp flour and cook for about 1 minute. Gradually add the stock and wine, stirring until thickened and smooth. Add 75 ml/ 5 tbsp of the parsley and the petits pois and season with salt and pepper.

5 Pour the sauce over the fried fish, and bake in the preheated oven for 15–20 minutes, adding the clams to the dish 3–4 minutes before the end of the cooking time.

6 Discard any clams that do not open, then sprinkle with the remaining chopped fresh parsley before serving.

Zarzuela

Zarzuela means "light opera" or "musical comedy" in Spanish and the classic fish stew of the same name should be just as lively and colourful.

Serves 6

INGREDIENTS
1 cooked lobster
1 large monkfish tail
225 g/8 oz squid rings
15 ml/1 tbsp plain flour
90 ml/6 tbsp olive oil
12 large raw prawns
2 large mild onions, chopped
4 garlic cloves, crushed
30 ml/2 tbsp brandy
450 g/1 lb ripe tomatoes, peeled and
    roughly chopped
2 bay leaves
5 ml/1 tsp paprika
1 red chilli, seeded and chopped
300 ml/½ pint/1¼ cups
    fish stock
24 fresh mussels or clams, debearded
    and scrubbed
15 g/½ oz/2 tbsp ground almonds
30 ml/2 tbsp chopped fresh parsley
salt and freshly ground
    black pepper

1 Using a large knife, cut the lobster in half lengthways. Remove the dark intestine that runs down the length of the tail. Crack the claws using a hammer. Cut the monkfish fillets away from the central cartilage and cut each fillet into three. Toss the monkfish and squid in seasoned flour.

2 Heat the oil in a frying pan. Add the monkfish and squid and fry until just soft, then remove from the pan. Fry the prawns until cooked, then remove from the pan.

3 Add the onions and two-thirds of the garlic and fry for 3 minutes. Add the brandy and ignite. When the flames die down, add the tomatoes, bay leaves, paprika, chilli and stock.

4 Bring to the boil, reduce the heat and simmer gently for 5 minutes. Add the mussels or clams, cover and cook for 3–4 minutes, until the shells have opened, then remove from the pan.

5 Discard any mussels or clams that remain closed. Arrange all the fish, including the lobster, in a large, flameproof serving dish.

6 Blend the ground almonds to a paste with the remaining garlic and parsley and stir into the sauce. Season with salt and pepper. Pour the sauce over the fish and lobster and cook gently for about 8 minutes, until hot. Serve immediately.

Chicken Casserole with Spiced Figs

The Catalans have various recipes for fruit with meat. This is quite an unusual one, using one of the fruits most strongly associated with Spain – the fig, which is poached in a lightly spiced syrup.

Serves 4

INGREDIENTS
120 ml/4 fl oz/½ cup medium-sweet
    white wine
pared rind of ½ lemon
1.5 kg/3–3½ lb chicken, jointed into
    8 pieces
50 g/2 oz lardons, or thick bacon
    cut into strips
15 ml/1 tbsp olive oil
50 ml/2 fl oz/¼ cup chicken stock, boiling
salt and freshly ground
    black pepper
green salad, to serve

FOR THE FIGS
150 g/5 oz/⅔ cup sugar
120 ml/4 fl oz/½ cup white
    wine vinegar
1 lemon slice
1 cinnamon stick
450 g/1 lb fresh figs

1 To prepare the figs, put the sugar, vinegar, lemon slice and cinnamon stick in a pan with 120 ml/4 fl oz/ ½ cup water. Bring to the boil, then simmer for 5 minutes.

2 Add the figs to the syrup in the pan, cover, and simmer for a further 10 minutes. Remove the pan from the heat, and leave, covered, for 3 hours.

3 Preheat the oven to 180°C/350°F/ Gas 4. Drain the figs, and place them in a bowl. Add the wine and lemon rind. Season the chicken.

4 In a large frying pan, cook the lardons or bacon strips until the fat melts and they turn golden. Transfer to a shallow ovenproof dish, leaving any fat in the pan. Add the oil to the pan and brown the chicken pieces all over.

COOK'S TIP: Fresh figs are ripe when they feel soft to the touch and the skin has a bloom to it.

5 Drain the figs, adding the wine to the pan with the chicken. Boil until the sauce has reduced and is syrupy. Transfer the contents of the frying pan to the ovenproof dish and cook in the oven, uncovered, for about 20 minutes.

6 Add the figs and boiling chicken stock, cover the dish and return to the oven for a further 10 minutes or until the chicken feels cooked through when pierced with the tip of a sharp knife. Serve with a green salad.

Chicken with Chorizo

The addition of chorizo sausage and sherry gives a warm, interesting flavour to this simple casserole. Serve with rice or boiled potatoes.

Serves 4

INGREDIENTS
1 medium chicken, jointed, or 4 chicken
  legs, halved
10 ml/2 tsp paprika
60 ml/4 tbsp olive oil
2 small onions, sliced
6 garlic cloves, thinly sliced
150 g/5 oz chorizo sausage, sliced
400 g/14 oz can chopped tomatoes
12–16 fresh bay leaves
75 ml/5 tbsp medium sherry
salt and freshly ground black pepper
rice or potatoes, to serve

1 Preheat the oven to 190°C/375°F/ Gas 5. Coat the chicken pieces in the paprika, making sure they are evenly covered, then season with salt.

2 Heat the olive oil in a large frying pan and fry the chicken until browned all over, turning occasionally.

3 Transfer the chicken pieces to an ovenproof dish. Add the onions to the pan and fry quickly. Add the garlic and sliced chorizo and fry for 2 minutes.

4 Add the tomatoes, two bay leaves and the sherry and bring to the boil. Pour over the chicken and cover with a lid. Bake for 45 minutes.

5 Remove the lid and season to taste. Cook, uncovered, for 20 minutes, until the chicken is tender and golden. Serve with rice or potatoes, garnished with the remaining bay leaves.

Chicken with Ham & Olives

A colourful one-pot dish, ideal for entertaining, served with a green salad.

Serves 8

INGREDIENTS
30 ml/2 tbsp plain flour
10 ml/2 tsp paprika
2.5 ml/½ tsp salt
16 chicken drumsticks
60 ml/4 tbsp olive oil
1.2 litres/2 pints/5 cups chicken stock
1 onion, finely chopped
2 garlic cloves, crushed
450 g/1 lb/2⅓ cups long grain rice
2 bay leaves
225 g/8 oz/1⅓ cups diced *jamón serrano*
115 g/4 oz/1 cup pimiento-stuffed
    green olives
1 green pepper, seeded and diced
2 x 400 g/14 oz cans chopped tomatoes
60 ml/4 tbsp chopped fresh parsley
parsley sprig, to garnish

1 Preheat the oven to 180°C/350°F/ Gas 4. Shake together the flour, paprika and salt in a plastic bag, add the drumsticks and toss to coat. Heat the oil in a large, flameproof casserole and brown the chicken slowly on both sides. Remove and keep warm.

2 Add the stock to the casserole, boil and add the onion, garlic, rice and bay leaves. Cook for 10 minutes. Draw to the side of the casserole and add the next five ingredients. Stir to combine.

3 Arrange the chicken on top, cover and bake for 30-40 minutes, or until tender. Add more stock if necessary to prevent it from drying out. Remove the bay leaves and serve garnished with parsley.

Spiced Duck with Pears

This delicious casserole is based on a Catalan dish that uses goose or duck.

Serves 6

INGREDIENTS

6 duck portions, either breast or
    leg pieces
45 ml/3 tbsp olive oil
1 large onion, thinly sliced
1 cinnamon stick, halved
2 thyme sprigs
475 ml/16 fl oz/2 cups
    chicken stock
3 firm ripe pears
2 garlic cloves, sliced
25 g/1 oz/¼ cup pine nuts
2.5 ml/½ tsp saffron strands
25 g/1 oz/2 tbsp raisins
salt and freshly ground black pepper
parsley or young thyme sprigs,
    to garnish
mashed potatoes and green vegetables,
    to serve (optional)

1 Preheat the oven to 180°C/350°F/
Gas 4. Fry the duck in 15 ml/1 tbsp of
the oil for about 5 minutes, until the
skin is golden. Transfer the duck to an
ovenproof dish.

2 Drain off all but 15 ml/1 tbsp of
the fat in the pan, add the onion and
fry for 5 minutes. Add the cinnamon
stick, thyme and stock and bring to
the boil. Pour over the duck and bake
in the oven for 1¼ hours.

3 Meanwhile, halve the pears and fry
quickly in the remaining oil until
beginning to turn golden on the cut
sides. Pound the garlic, pine nuts and
saffron in a mortar with a pestle to
make a thick paste.

4 Add the paste to the casserole,
together with the raisins and pears.
Bake for a further 15 minutes until the
pears are tender.

5 Check the seasoning and add salt and pepper to taste, then garnish with parsley or thyme. Serve with mashed potatoes and a green vegetable, if liked.

COOK'S TIP: A good stock is essential for this dish. Buy a large duck (plus two extra duck breasts if you want portions to be generous) and joint it yourself, using the giblets and carcass for stock. Alternatively buy duck portions and a carton of chicken stock.

Lamb with Red Peppers & Rioja

Plenty of garlic, peppers, herbs and red wine give this lamb stew a lovely rich flavour. Slice through the pepper stalks, rather than removing them.

Serves 4

INGREDIENTS
900 g/2 lb lean lamb fillet
15 ml/1 tbsp plain flour
60 ml/4 tbsp olive oil
2 red onions, sliced
4 garlic cloves, sliced
10 ml/2 tsp paprika
1.5 ml/¼ tsp ground cloves
2 fresh bay leaves
2 thyme sprigs
400 ml/14 fl oz/1⅔ cups red Rioja
150 ml/¼ pint/⅔ cup lamb stock
3 red peppers, halved and seeded
salt and freshly ground black pepper
fresh bay leaves and thyme sprigs, to garnish
green beans and saffron rice or boiled
    potatoes, to serve

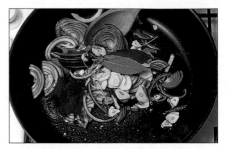

2 Heat the oil in a frying pan and fry the lamb, stirring, until browned. Transfer to an ovenproof dish. Fry the onions in the pan with the garlic, paprika, cloves, bay leaves and thyme.

3 Add the Rioja and stock and bring to the boil, stirring. Pour the contents of the pan over the meat. Cover with a lid and bake for 30 minutes.

4 Remove the dish from the oven. Stir the red peppers into the stew and season lightly with salt and pepper. Bake for a further 30 minutes, until the meat is tender. Garnish the stew with bay leaves and sprigs of thyme and serve with green beans and saffron rice or boiled potatoes.

1 Preheat the oven to 160°C/325°F/ Gas 3. Cut the lamb into chunks. Season the flour, add the lamb and toss lightly to coat.

VARIATION: Use any lean cubed pork instead of the lamb and a white Rioja instead of the red.

Pork & Sausage Casserole

This pork dish from the Catalan region uses spicy butifarra sausages. You can find them in some Spanish delicatessens but, if not, sweet Italian sausages will also taste excellent in this recipe.

Serves 4

INGREDIENTS
30 ml/2 tbsp olive oil
4 boneless pork chops, about 175 g/6 oz
4 butifarra or sweet Italian sausages
1 onion, chopped
2 garlic cloves, chopped
120 ml/4 fl oz/½ cup dry white wine
4 plum tomatoes, chopped
1 bay leaf
30 ml/2 tbsp chopped fresh parsley
salt and freshly ground black pepper
green salad, to serve

2 Add the sausages, onion and garlic to the pan and cook over a moderate heat until the sausages are browned and the onion softened, turning the sausages two or three times during cooking. Return the chops to the pan.

1 Heat the oil in a large, deep frying pan. Cook the pork chops over a high heat until browned on both sides, then transfer to a plate.

VARIATION: Vine tomatoes, which are making a welcome appearance in our supermarkets, can be used instead of plum tomatoes.

3 Stir in the wine, tomatoes and bay leaf and season with salt and pepper. Add the parsley. Cover the pan and cook for 30 minutes.

4 Remove the sausages from the pan and cut into thick slices. Return them to the pan and heat through. Serve hot, accompanied by a green salad.

Meatballs in Tomato Sauce

These delicious little meatballs in their aromatic sauce may be served with pasta or rice for a filling lunch dish.

Serves 4

INGREDIENTS
225 g/8 oz minced beef
 or lamb
4 spring onions, thinly sliced
2 garlic cloves, finely chopped
30 ml/2 tbsp freshly grated mature
 Manchego cheese
10 ml/2 tsp fresh thyme leaves
15 ml/1 tbsp olive oil
3 tomatoes, chopped
30 ml/2 tbsp red or dry
 white wine
10 ml/2 tsp chopped fresh rosemary
pinch of sugar
salt and freshly ground
 black pepper
fresh thyme, to garnish

2 Mix thoroughly, then shape the mixture into 12 small firm balls, using your fingers.

3 Heat the olive oil in a large frying pan and cook the meatballs, turning frequently, for 5 minutes, until evenly browned all over.

COOK'S TIP: Mature Manchego cheese is now widely available from large supermarkets as well as speciality cheese shops.

1 Place the minced beef or lamb in a bowl. Add the spring onions, garlic, Manchego and thyme and plenty of salt and pepper.

4 Add the chopped tomatoes, wine, rosemary and sugar, with salt and pepper to taste. Cover and cook gently for 15 minutes, until the tomatoes are pulpy and the meatballs are cooked. Serve hot, garnished with thyme.

Iced Oranges

Oranges are almost synonymous with Spain, and what more refreshing
way to serve them than these attractive sorbets?

Serves 8

INGREDIENTS
150 g/5 oz/¾ cup sugar, plus extra,
    if required
juice of 1 lemon, plus extra, if required
14 medium oranges
an extra orange or bought orange juice,
    if necessary
8 fresh bay leaves, to decorate

1 Put the sugar in a heavy-based pan.
Add half the lemon juice, and
120 ml/4 fl oz/½ cup water. Cook
over a low heat until the sugar has
dissolved. Bring to the boil and boil,
stirring, for 2–3 minutes, until the
syrup is clear. Leave to cool.

2 Slice the tops off eight of the
oranges, to make "hats". Scoop out the
flesh with a teaspoon and reserve. Put
the hollowed-out orange shells and
"hats" on a tray and place in the
freezer until needed.

3 Finely grate the rind of the
remaining oranges and add to the
syrup. Squeeze the juice from the
oranges, and from the reserved flesh.
There should be 750 ml/1¼ pints/3
cups. Squeeze another orange or add
bought orange juice, if necessary.

4 Stir the orange juice and remaining
lemon juice, with 90 ml/6 tbsp water,
into the syrup. Taste, adding more
lemon juice or sugar, as desired. Pour
the mixture into a shallow freezer
container and freeze for 3 hours.

5 Turn the mixture into a bowl, and
whisk to break down the ice crystals.
Freeze for 4 hours more, until firm,
but not solid.

6 Pack the mixture into the orange
shells and set the "hats" on top. Freeze
until ready to serve. Just before
serving, push a skewer into the tops of
the "hats" and push in a bay leaf.

Poached Pears in Red Wine

The sweet, fruity, almost vanilla flavour of Rioja makes it the perfect wine for these marvellous poached pears.

Serves 6

INGREDIENTS
6 eating pears
750 ml/1¼ pints/3 cups
    Rioja
105 ml/7 tbsp caster sugar
2 cinnamon sticks
6 bay leaves, to decorate

2 Slice 5 mm/¼ in off the bottom of each pear so that it will stand upright. Stand the pears in a saucepan that will hold them comfortably but snugly. Add the sugar, wine and cinnamon sticks.

1 Peel the pears, leaving the stalks intact. Push the end of a swivel-blade vegetable peeler into the base of each pear to a depth of about 4 cm/1½ in. Twist and remove the core.

COOK'S TIP: Check the pears are tender by piercing each one with a sharp knife towards the end of the poaching time, because some may cook more quickly than others.

3 Bring the wine to the boil, cover, lower the heat and simmer for about 15–20 minutes, until the pears are tender. Transfer the pears to a dish and keep hot. Boil the wine syrup until reduced by half.

4 Strain the syrup and pour it over the pears. Serve immediately, decorated with the bay leaves, or chill and serve cold, if preferred.

Flan

Although it originated in Spain, this dessert has been adopted by French cuisine as crème caramel and is now served throughout the world.

Serves 6–8

INGREDIENTS
250 g/9 oz/1¼ cups sugar
60 ml/4 tbsp water
1 vanilla pod or 10 ml/2 tsp vanilla essence
400 ml/14 fl oz/1⅔ cups milk
250 ml/8 fl oz/1 cup whipping cream
5 large eggs
2 egg yolks

1 Put 175 g/6 oz/scant 1 cup of the sugar in a small, heavy saucepan with the water. Bring to the boil over a high heat, swirling the pan to dissolve the sugar. Boil, without stirring, for 4–5 minutes, until the syrup turns a dark caramel colour.

2 Immediately pour the caramel into a 1 litre/1⅔ pint/4 cup soufflé dish. Quickly swirl the dish to coat the base and sides with the caramel then place the dish in a small roasting tin.

3 Preheat the oven to 160°C/325°F/ Gas 3. With a small, sharp knife, split the vanilla pod lengthways, if using, and scrape the black seeds into a medium saucepan. Add the milk and cream and bring just to the boil over a medium heat, stirring frequently. Remove the pan from the heat, cover and set aside for 15–20 minutes. Alternatively, mix the vanilla essence with the milk and cream and heat.

4 In a bowl, whisk the eggs and egg yolks with the remaining sugar for 2–3 minutes, until smooth and creamy. Whisk in the hot milk and carefully strain the mixture into the caramel-lined dish. Cover with foil.

5 Pour enough boiling water into the roasting tin to come halfway up the sides of the dish. Bake the custard for 40–45 minutes, until a knife inserted about 5 cm/2 in from the edge comes out clean. Remove from the roasting tin, cool, then chill overnight.

6 To turn out, run a sharp knife around the edge of the dish. Cover the dish with a serving plate and invert. Gently lift one edge of the dish, allowing the caramel to run over the sides, then gently lift off the dish.

COOK'S TIP: Cooking the flan in a roasting tin of water, or bain-marie, enables the custard to be cooked gently without curdling.

Orange Rice Pudding

In Spain, rice puddings are a favourite dish, especially when sweetened with honey and flavoured with orange.

Serves 4

INGREDIENTS
50 g/2 oz/4 tbsp short grain pudding rice
600 ml/1 pint/2½ cups milk
30–45 ml/2–3 tbsp clear honey
   (according to taste)
finely grated rind of ½ small orange
150 ml/¼ pint/⅔ cup double cream
15 ml/1 tbsp chopped pistachio nuts or
   blanched almonds, toasted

1 Mix the rice with the milk, honey and orange rind in a saucepan and bring to the boil. Reduce the heat, cover and simmer very gently for about 1¼ hours, stirring regularly.

2 Remove the lid and continue cooking and stirring the rice mixture for about 15–20 minutes, until the rice is creamy but still with a bit of bite.

3 Pour in the double cream and simmer for 5–8 minutes longer until just soft. Serve the rice sprinkled with the pistachio nuts or almonds in individual warmed bowls.

COOK'S TIP: Single flower honeys have a much more distinctive flavour than blended honeys. For a really authentic – and perfectly delicious – dish, use orange blossom honey.

Figs & Pears in Honey

A stunningly simple dessert which uses two Mediterranean favourites – fresh figs and pears.

Serves 4

INGREDIENTS
1 lemon
90 ml/6 tbsp
    clear honey
1 cinnamon stick
1 cardamom pod
350 ml/12 fl oz/1½ cups water
2 pears
8 fresh figs, halved

1 Pare the rind from the lemon using a zester or vegetable peeler, and cut into very thin strips.

2 Place the lemon rind, honey, cinnamon stick, cardamom pod and water in a pan and boil, uncovered, for about 10 minutes, until reduced by about half.

3 Cut the pears into eighths, discarding the core. Leave the peel on or peel as preferred. Place in the syrup, add the figs and simmer for about 5 minutes, until tender.

4 Transfer the fruit to a bowl. Cook the liquid until syrupy, then discard the cinnamon stick and pour over the fruit.

Crema Catalana

This delicious Spanish pudding is not as rich as a crème brûlée, but has a similar caramelized sugar topping.

Serves 4

INGREDIENTS
475 ml/16 fl oz/2 cups milk
pared rind of ½ lemon
1 cinnamon stick
4 egg yolks
105 ml/7 tbsp caster sugar
25 ml/1½ tbsp cornflour
freshly grated nutmeg

1 Put the milk in a pan with the lemon rind and cinnamon stick. Bring to the boil, then allow to simmer for 10 minutes. Remove the lemon rind and cinnamon. Place the egg yolks and 45 ml/3 tbsp of the sugar in a bowl and whisk until pale yellow. Add the cornflour and mix well.

COOK'S TIP: The dessert should be served very soon after the topping has caramelized. The caramel will stay hard for only about 30 minutes.

2 Stir in a few tablespoons of the hot milk, then add this mixture to the remaining milk. Return to the heat and cook gently, stirring, for about 5 minutes, until thickened and smooth. Do not allow to boil.

3 Pour the custard mixture into four shallow ovenproof dishes, about 13 cm/ 5 in in diameter. Leave to cool, then chill for a few hours, overnight if possible, until firm.

4 Just before you are ready to serve, sprinkle each pudding with 15 ml/ 1 tbsp sugar and a little grated nutmeg. Preheat the grill to high.

5 Place the chilled puddings under the hot grill, on the highest shelf, and cook them until the sugar topping caramelizes by turning brown and crunchy. This will take only a few seconds. Leave the desserts to cool for a few minutes before serving.

VARIATION: An alternative way of caramelizing the topping is to heat the back of a spoon and press it down on the topping until it turns crunchy. Repeat, wiping and reheating the spoon each time.

This edition is published by Hermes House

Hermes House is an imprint of Anness Publishing Limited,

Hermes House,
88–89 Blackfriars Road,
London SE1 8HA

Publisher: Joanna Lorenz
Editor: Valerie Ferguson
Series Designer: Bobbie Colgate Stone
Designer: Andrew Heath
Editorial Reader: Penelope Goodare
Production Controller: Joanna King
Recipes contributed by: Catherine Atkinson, Janet Brinkworth, Sarah Edmonds,
Joanna Farrow, Silvano Franco, Sarah Gates, Shirley Gill
Photography: Karl Adamson, Steve Baxter, James Duncan, Michelle Garrett,
Patrick McLeavey, Thomas Odulate

3 5 7 9 10 8 6 4

Notes:
For all recipes, quantities are given in both metric and imperial measures and, where
appropriate, measures are also given in standard cups and spoons.
Follow one set, but not a mixture, because they are not interchangeable.

Standard spoon and cup measures are level.

1 tsp = 5 ml   1 tbsp =15 ml   1 cup = 250 ml/8 fl oz

Australian standard tablespoons are 20 ml.
Australian readers should use 3 tsp in place of 1 tbsp for measuring small quantities of
gelatine, cornflour, salt, etc.

Medium eggs are used unless otherwise stated.

Printed in China